History of Britain
Book 3

HENRY VII TO GEORGE III

1485-1783
Philip Sauvain

Macmillan Education

Introduction

When the Welshman, Henry Tudor, defeated and killed Richard III at the Battle of Bosworth in 1485, he brought to an end the disastrous Wars of the Roses, which had been fought between rival supporters of the families of Lancaster and York.

Henry Tudor was a Lancastrian, but when he was crowned Henry VII he helped to bring peace to England by marrying Elizabeth, daughter of the Yorkist king Edward IV. Henry VII, his son Henry VIII, and grandchildren Edward VI, Mary I and Elizabeth I, were known as the **Tudors**, and reigned throughout the 16th century.

Elizabeth died in 1603 and was succeeded by James VI of Scotland (the great-great-grandson of Henry VII), who came to the throne as James I. So began the **Stuart** period. This too, lasted just over a hundred years, ending in 1714 when a German prince (James I's great-grandson) became the first of the four kings, called George, who reigned from 1714 to 1830.

In the 300 years from 1485 Britain changed – from a fairly unimportant island to a country about to become the world's first industrial nation and the centre of the most powerful empire on earth.

Much of this success was due to the strong government of the Tudors. Many lords had been killed in the Wars of the Roses and after 1485 the nobility no longer had the power and influence it once held in the Middle Ages. When Henry VII died in 1509 Britain was at peace and beginning to build up an important fleet of merchant ships.

Contents

The Tudors

King Henry VIII

New Year's Eve 1510. Everyone in the Royal Palace at Richmond hoped the baby would be a boy. Not long after midnight came the news they had all been waiting for. Queen Catherine of England had given birth to a boy called Henry – a future Henry IX. The news spread rapidly, and huge bonfires were lit in the streets in celebration.

King Henry VIII in about 1520 when he was a young man aged 30

Philip of Spain and Mary Tudor (Henry VIII's elder daughter)

Edward VI (Henry VIII's son)

Then two months later the baby prince died. For a time there was grief, but then people told themselves the Queen would soon have other children. Catherine, a daughter of the King of Spain, had originally married Henry VIII's elder brother Arthur, but Arthur died in 1502 so she married Henry.

Henry became king in 1509 and was well-liked by the people. He was every inch a king – good-looking, strong, clever and good at sport.

But then things began to go wrong with his life. Although Catherine gave birth to several children, they all died except Princess Mary. Henry badly wanted a son to be the next King of England. He began to think that God was punishing him for marrying Arthur's wife. As a Catholic he knew he could not get a divorce. So his chief minister Cardinal Wolsey asked the Pope to annul (cancel) the marriage, because the Bible said that a man should not marry his brother's widow.

But the Pope would not agree. Henry was so furious that he dismissed Wolsey. By this time he had fallen in love with Anne Boleyn, a young lady who first caught his eye when she came to court in 1522. Thomas Cromwell, the new chief minister, suggested that if Henry took control of the Church himself, the marriage to Catherine could then be annulled by the Archbishop of Canterbury and he would be free to marry Anne. Besides, many people complained about the way the Church was being run.

Henry thought this was the best thing to do. So he married Anne Boleyn, and got Parliament to say he was now the Supreme Head of the Church of England.

But the new marriage was no better than the first. Anne gave birth to a baby girl called Elizabeth (who later became queen). But Henry still demanded a son. After Anne's second baby was stillborn she was put on trial and executed.

Two weeks later Henry married his third wife, Jane Seymour, but she died soon after giving birth to a boy called Edward. However, at last he had a son to succeed him to the throne.

Henry VIII had three more wives after that – Anne of Cleves, Catherine Howard and Catherine Parr. But Edward was his only son.

The Dissolution of the Monasteries

There were still many people in England who did not accept Henry VIII as Head of the Church, and stayed loyal to the Pope. Sir Thomas More and some other men who thought like this were accused of treason and executed.

Henry wanted to make the Church less powerful. Many complaints had been made about the behaviour of the monks at this time, so Henry made this his excuse for taking their land. Inspectors were sent to the monasteries. They reported, unfairly, that the monasteries were often wicked places, and should be closed. In those days the Church owned one-third of the land in England. Henry shut the monasteries and took away their land.

Many abbeys, together with their rich farmland, were sold to raise money, and some of the buildings became farmhouses or mansions. Many were pulled down or fell into ruins.

Poor people were hit hard by the closure of the monasteries, for the monks had often given them food and shelter. But a protest march in the north of England, called the **Pilgrimage of Grace**, was put down and the ringleaders were executed.

The closure of a monastery

Queen Elizabeth I in a procession through London

Queen Elizabeth I

Queen Elizabeth I

Edward VI succeeded his father as King, but died when he was only 16. Edward was a strong Protestant, and while he lived, church services began to be spoken in English for the first time.

When Edward died Mary, his half-sister, became queen. She was Catherine of Aragon's daughter, and a strong Catholic. She had many Protestants put to death, including the Archbishop of Canterbury. She even imprisoned her own sister Elizabeth, fearing she might be plotting against her.

Queen Mary reigned for only five years, and then died. When Elizabeth became Queen, bonfires blazed in the streets to celebrate the return of a Protestant monarch once more. Elizabeth soon became very popular. She made many visits to different parts of England and often went in procession, riding in a coach, or in a litter carried by her attendants at court.

Elizabeth never married, although many men would have liked to have been her husband. When she came to the throne people thought of Britain as a small and unimportant island. When she died, 45 years later, her navy had defeated the mighty Spanish Armada and England controlled the seas. Explorers like Drake and Raleigh had sailed round the world and founded settlements in America. Great painters, musicians and writers flourished in Elizabethan England, including the great playwright William Shakespeare.

Mary, Queen of Scots

There was a darker side to Elizabeth's reign, however. Some Catholics claimed that she was not the rightful heir to the throne. They said that her mother Anne Boleyn was never really the queen, and the crown should go to Mary, Queen of Scots, a Catholic, who had been Queen of Scotland since 1542.

Mary had an exciting but rather unhappy life. In 1565 she married her cousin Lord Darnley, but soon tired of him and became very friendly with her secretary, David Rizzio. This made Darnley so angry that he broke into Holyrood Palace and stabbed Rizzio to death in front of the Queen. Mary got her revenge when Darnley fell ill and was strangely blown up by a gunpowder explosion.

The Earl of Bothwell was accused of the murder but acquitted; so when he married Mary three months later, the Scots were scandalised. Mary was taken prisoner and forced to give up the throne of Scotland in favour of her son, James VI. She escaped to England but was taken prisoner, and held a captive in English castles for twenty years.

The murder of Rizzio

A number of unsuccessful plots against Elizabeth were hatched in that time. Then in 1586, letters were found which appeared to show that Mary had agreed that Queen Elizabeth should be killed. This was treason if true, and on 1st February 1587 Mary was beheaded at Fotheringhay Castle.

Things To Do

1. "His majesty is extremely handsome. He is very fair and has a beard that looks like gold. He is very accomplished, a good musician, a most excellent horseman, a fine jouster, speaks good French, Latin, and Spanish, is very religious, very fond of hunting, and extremely fond of tennis. He is good tempered, harms no one, and is very rich." This was what an Italian thought of Henry VIII in 1519. Write another description of Henry VIII in 1547, taking into account all the things he did during his reign.

2. Why did Henry VIII (a) divorce Catherine of Aragon (b) close the monasteries (c) make himself Head of the Church of England? Do you think he was right to do so?

3. Draw or paint a picture to show Queen Elizabeth carried in procession through the crowded streets of London.

Afterwards

Queen Elizabeth died in 1603 without a son or daughter to succeed to the throne. So James VI of Scotland became King of England as James I. He was a member of the Stewart family in Scotland, so the new Kings of England were called Stuarts.

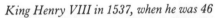
King Henry VIII in 1537, when he was 46

Daily Life in Elizabethan England

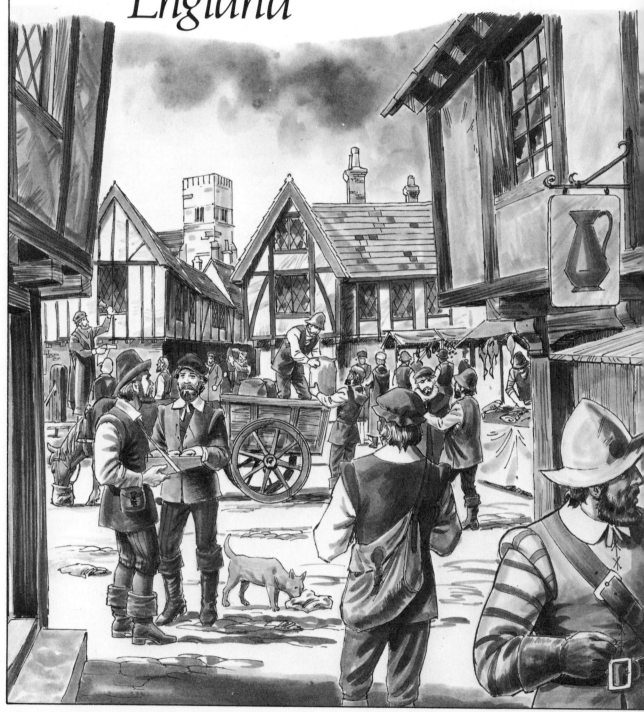

Early morning in an Elizabethan street

It is the middle of a summer's night in the narrow streets of Elizabethan London, about four hundred years ago. The alleyways are dark and forbidding, and it is easy to imagine shadowy figures in the gloom. The upper storeys of the houses jut out over the streets, making them dark even in the moonlight.

The bellman walks slowly along, crying "One o'clock and all's well!" Sometimes he shouts when he sees a candle burning, telling the maids inside to make sure their doors are locked and that the fire and lights are out. In one street a barking dog frightens off a burglar, and brings the watchman running. There are no policemen, so soldiers are put on watch duty every night to patrol the streets.

Time passes. It is now 3 a.m. and some candles are being lit. Near the town fields the milkmaids are up, and will soon be out to milk the cows. In some houses a huge pot of porridge is ready for the servants' breakfast at 4 a.m.

A faint glimmer of sun gets bigger, and with the dawn the soldiers on watch go home. At 5 a.m. church bells start to ring, calling people to early services. The streets fill up with people. In many homes, schoolboys are getting ready, in a hurry to be off to school.

Women are already out in the gardens, feeding the chickens and pigs while carts, laden high with vegetables and fruit, roll through the streets.

Soon after six o'clock the shops open. Wooden shutters are taken down and goods displayed on the counters. Each shop has a sign outside to show its trade. In the market place, country people set out their goods and start to shout their wares. Two boys dash through the streets, knowing they will be beaten if they are late for school.

By 7 a.m. everyone is busy at work, and by 8 a.m. people begin to eat breakfast. This is a simple meal of bread and beer. By nine o'clock the market place is packed with people, and the shops are full of customers. Apprentices cry out their wares, "What d'ye lack? Fine Cloth! Hot pies!" The town crier shouts out the day's notices. In Tudor times there were no newspapers, so the only way people heard local news was from the town crier.

At dinner

In many homes, servants are already preparing dinner. A passer-by, looking through the window in a merchant's home, sees maids folding napkins, cleaning knives and laying the table. In the kitchen cooks are busy roasting meat, cooking vegetables and baking bread.

By 11 a.m. work stops and the children come home from school for a simple meal of porridge or bread and cheese. In his large house a rich man sits down to a dinner of beef, chicken, mackerel, eels, strawberries and cream, oranges, lemons, cherries and sweetmeats. The shop assistants also go for dinner now, whilst their masters look after the shop.

The afternoon passes. At 3 p.m. a wedding procession can be seen in the market place, with the bride in ribbons, attended by pages, musicians, and maids of honour carrying bride-cakes and garlands of wheat, as they enter the great church at the side of the square.

It is now late afternoon, but there is no sign of the shops shutting yet. At 5 p.m. the boys are let out of school and play in the streets, their satchels lying in the dirt.

At school

Early evening, and the workmen and apprentices look forward to closing time at 7 p.m., when the counters go up, and the wooden shutters are fastened tight. The streets are quieter now, but tavern doors sometimes bang open and a drunk falls into the street. As dusk falls, the soldiers of the watch get ready for the night's work, and the bellman starts his rounds once more.

On the roads outside the town, beggars and vagabonds can be seen, shuffling along the highways. Many are poor farmworkers, who lost their jobs when some landowners turned their fields and common lands into sheep pastures. It is cheaper to employ one shepherd than several farmworkers: and there is money to be made from wool, for the clothing industry is doing well.

Queen Elizabeth and her ministers have tried to do something about the poverty in the country by making each parish build a *poor house*, where the unemployed can be given work. The cost of running the poor house is found by collecting a tax called a *poor-rate*. But not all the beggars want work. Some are thieves and vagabonds, such as the *dummerers*, who pretend to be dumb, and the *priggers of prancers* (horse-thieves). The government has passed laws, saying that sturdy beggars who will not work, are to be whipped, and then branded with a hot iron.

Beggars and vagabonds near a village

Weaving

A Tudor forge

There are many new crafts, but the manufacture of cloth is still the main industry. Most weavers and spinners work in small workshops and cottages, but one clothier is said to have 200 men weavers at work in one room, and 300 women spinning and carding wool in another.

In the north of England there are coal pits, where the miners dig a tunnel into the side of a hill to get the coal out, or else dig a short shaft and cut away all the coal at the bottom before moving on to another pit. There are often accidents. If the shafts are dug too deep, they flood easily when it rains. Sometimes there are rock falls and explosions.

In woodland places, iron ore is smelted in furnaces which burn charcoal. The hot iron is hammered into shape on an *anvil*. At some forges a waterwheel is connected to a huge *tilt hammer*. As the wheel goes round, it lifts the heavy hammer up and down and its great power is used to shape the largest slabs of iron.

14

An Elizabethan theatre – the Swan Theatre in London, 1596

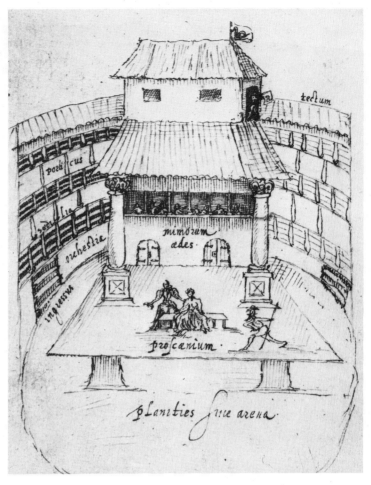

London is growing fast, and some land which was green fields and meadows at the time of Henry VIII is now "a continual building of garden-houses and small cottages".

Bowling-alleys, gambling houses and theatres have been built. Across London Bridge, in Southwark, there are "two bear gardens, wherein be kept bears, bulls, and other beasts, to be baited." Bears, tied in chains, are attacked by fierce dogs.

In the afternoons a flag flies over the newly-opened Globe Theatre, where a play is being performed on a stage jutting out into the audience. There is little scenery, so the actors bring branches on to the stage to show a forest, or tankards for an inn. The costumes are very colourful, especially those of the boys, who take the women's parts.

Outside in the streets, boys kick a football around. An onlooker says it is "a friendly kind of fight, sometimes their necks are broken, sometimes their backs."

Labels on illustration: withdrawing room, long gallery, great chamber, chamber, great hall, parlour

A Tudor mansion

Four hundred years later, many reminders of daily life in Elizabethan England can still be seen. Tudor mansions, like Montacute House in Somerset, help us to imagine how rich people lived then. Many of these mansions were built of brick with tall chimneys and glass windows.

They usually had a Great Hall on the ground floor, where guests were received, and where the servants had their meals. The owners of the mansion had their meals in the Parlour next door, a smaller and cosier room which was their main living room. They entertained guests in the Great Chamber or Presence Room on the first floor, and above this on the second floor was the Long Gallery – a huge room, stretching the length of the mansion. Children played here when it rained, while adults strolled in conversation. Minstrels and strolling players put on their shows here.

Above the Long Gallery were the attic rooms where the servants slept. In those days servants were paid such low wages that a rich man could afford to employ hundreds of them.

The furniture was very heavy and made from solid oak. The owner and his important guests slept in four-poster beds, each with a curtain rail, so,that curtains could be drawn round the bed at night to give privacy and warmth.

Things To Do

1. Draw a sequence of pictures to tell the story of a day in the life of an Elizabethan town, starting with the bellman on his rounds in the early morning.

2. Look at the picture on page 15. Imagine you are visiting an Elizabethan theatre for the first time and write an account of the visit.

3. The photographs on this page were taken at a special display at Kentwell Hall in Suffolk, when people in the house wore Elizabethan clothes. Write two or three sentences to say what each picture shows. Would you have liked to have lived in Elizabethan England?

Afterwards

London grew rapidly in size. Many people built on to their existing houses in the city centre or dug cellars. As a result the streets became even more crowded and some parts of London were like a rabbit warren. Traffic increased, especially when hackney carriages and sedan chairs were introduced in about 1635. The streets were still filthy and littered with rubbish, and there were many outbreaks of disease and fires. In 1665–1666 there were two terrible disasters – the Plague and the Great Fire of London. Afterwards Londoners paid more attention to making their city a safer and healthier place to live in.

Tudor Seamen

Sir Francis Drake

Explorers

In the summer of 1572, an English sailor high up a tree in Panama looked out over the Pacific Ocean below him, where only Spanish ships sailed. He said later it gave him an overwhelming desire "to sail an English ship in that sea". The sailor was Francis Drake, then 32 years old.

The Spaniards had built ships on the Pacific shore of Central America, to carry gold and silver up the coast to a place from which it could be taken overland to an Atlantic port and so back home to Spain. Drake knew that the treasure ships were unarmed, because the Spanish thought it impossible for an enemy ship to sail into the Pacific.

But in 1577 Drake sailed from Plymouth in his ship *Pelican* to do just that. He sailed to South America first, and then through the Straits of Magellan into the Pacific, where he renamed his ship *Golden Hind*. After many adventures, looting treasure ships and plundering towns, he sailed up the coast and claimed California for Queen Elizabeth, calling it New Albion. It was there he first met Red Indians.

The 'Golden Hind' compared in size with the 'Queen Elizabeth 2'

Rather than face the Spanish warships waiting for him in the Atlantic, he returned across the Pacific, completing his round-the-world voyage on 26 September 1580. Six months later the Queen went to his ship and knighted him on the main deck, saying "Arise, Sir Francis Drake."

There were several other famous British explorers besides Drake. In 1497 John Cabot and his three sons sailed from Bristol in his ship *Mathew* and discovered Newfoundland and Canada – the first sailors to reach these countries since the Vikings.

The 'Golden Hind'

Sailors in Europe were trying to find a sea route to the riches of the Far East, because Moslems and Tartars had stopped merchants travelling there by land. Vasco da Gama, who was Portuguese, sailed to India round the Cape of Good Hope in South Africa, and Magellan's ship sailed round South America to the East Indies. Many European sailors thought there ought to be other ways to the north-east and north-west.

A British sailor called Richard Chancellor set sail from London in May 1553 in the ship *Bonaventure* and at last reached the coast of Russia at Archangel. Then he travelled overland by sledge to Moscow. Another great explorer called Martin Frobisher, tried a different route to the Indies, by sailing towards the north-west. In 1576 he sailed northwards, and avoiding icebergs (which he called "islands of ice"), arrived at the coast of Labrador in north Canada. There he saw Eskimos wearing furs and paddling canoes made of seal skin. Frobisher was later knighted by Queen Elizabeth.

The Spanish Armada

The Armada was a fleet of huge Spanish warships, sent by King Philip of Spain to invade England in 1588. Philip was a Catholic and hated Protestants; but what really persuaded him to send the Armada was the help Elizabeth had given to the enemies of Spain in the Netherlands, and also the raids by British seamen on Spanish treasure ships. He already had a large army in the Netherlands, so his Armada of 130 ships was sent to take them across the English Channel.

When the Armada was seen off the coast of Cornwall, bonfires (called beacons) were lit to tell everyone of the danger of invasion. Queen Elizabeth herself went down to Tilbury to meet her soldiers, wearing armour and telling them she too was prepared to fight and die for England. "I know I have the body of a weak and feeble woman," she said, "but I have the heart and stomach of a king and a king of England too."

However, the soldiers were not called upon to fight. The navy made sure the ships of the Armada never got near enough to carry out the threatened invasion. The Spanish ships were bigger than the English, but clumsier and not so well-armed. The English ships had twice as many large guns as the Spanish.

Drake, Frobisher and Hawkins were the leading English sea captains. They sailed out to harass the Spanish Armada as it sailed down the English Channel. There were few ships sunk on either side and the Armada anchored near Calais, with the ships still close together.

Then the English used an old trick of setting fire to some empty ships and letting them float towards the Armada. When the fireships appeared the commanders of the Spanish galleons panicked and, fearing their ships would catch fire and explode the gunpowder on board, hastily put to sea.

This was just what the English seamen had hoped for. The ships of the Armada were no longer together, so the English navy came in close and fired again and again at the lumbering Spanish ships. Several boats were sunk and many were shot to pieces, but then the wind changed and the Spaniards escaped into the North Sea.

Then the Spanish gave up any thought of invasion with their crippled fleet, and decided to return home to Spain by sailing northwards round the coasts of Scotland and Ireland. But strong winds and rough seas sank many ships on the journey home, and when they eventually reached Spain, they had lost half their ships and 20,000 men.

The defeat of the Spanish Armada was a resounding victory for the English navy. None of the English ships had been lost, and no more than a hundred men had fallen in battle. The exploits of daring seamen like Drake were admired all over Europe.

The Spanish Armada

A busy port in the eighteenth century

After Chancellor's voyage to Russia, the Muscovy Company was formed to trade with the Russians. In Canada, the voyages of Cabot and Frobisher were followed by those of Henry Hudson, and in the seventeenth century trading posts were set up in Canada by the Hudson's Bay Company. In 1600 the East India Company was founded to trade with India and the East Indies.

British ports soon bustled with activity as dockers unloaded spices, silks and other exotic goods from the Indies and the Americas. Ports, like Bristol, Ipswich and Southampton, thrived on the trade brought by these explorers and merchants.

The Spanish, Portuguese and French founded settlements in the lands they discovered and soon England followed suit. In 1584 Sir Walter Raleigh tried to establish a colony in an area he called Virginia after the Queen (popularly known as the Virgin Queen). Raleigh's colony failed, but he brought back two important new crops – tobacco and the potato. Virginia was later settled by Captain John Smith in the reign of King James I.

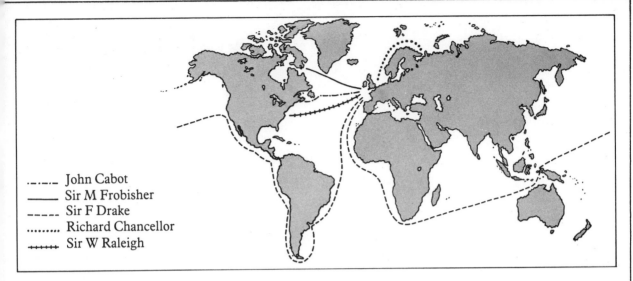

.—.— John Cabot
——— Sir M Frobisher
– – – Sir F Drake
········· Richard Chancellor
+–+–+ Sir W Raleigh

Journeys of exploration in the Sixteenth Century

Things To Do

1. Write one or two sentences, saying what you know about each of the following:

"Golden Hind" The Armada
Sir Walter Raleigh John Cabot
Richard Chancellor Sir Martin Frobisher

2. Draw or paint a picture of a sea fight between an English ship and a galleon of the Spanish Armada. Why was the Armada beaten?

3. What benefits came to Britain as a result of the voyages undertaken by English seamen in the Tudor period?

4. Copy the outline map of the world above, and find out from an atlas the names of the places visited by Drake, Chancellor, Cabot and Frobisher.

Afterwards

The defeat of the Spanish Armada showed people in Britain how important it was to have a strong navy. If Britain controlled the seas she could always stop an invasion force from landing. The first settlements overseas were followed by many more. British settlers went to live in North America, Africa, India, and much later in Australia and New Zealand. These small settlements eventually grew and became part of a huge British Empire. The settlers weren't always people hoping to get rich from trade or treasure. Those who settled in New England in America in 1620 were Puritans who wanted to follow their own religion in complete freedom.

King James I

The Gunpowder Plot

Making as little sound as possible, the conspirators rowed their dangerous cargo across the Thames towards Westminster. There they unloaded the barrels of gunpowder into a cellar underneath the House of Lords. Leaving Guy Fawkes to guard the cellar, they waited for the day when King James I would come to the House of Lords to open Parliament. They planned to blow him sky high.

They were Catholics, furious because King James refused to let them worship as they pleased. At that time Catholic priests were not allowed to say Mass, and everyone had to go to Church of England services.

Lord Monteagle and King James I reading the letter warning of the Gunpowder Plot

King James I   *Guy Fawkes*

But one of the conspirators was worried that Catholics would also die in the explosion and wrote an anonymous letter to Lord Monteagle, warning him not to attend the Opening of Parliament, since "they shall receive a terrible blow this parliament." Lord Monteagle showed the letter to James I, so the cellars under the House of Lords were searched.

At 11 at night on 4th November 1605, Guy Fawkes was discovered guarding what seemed like a pile of firewood. The soldiers looked underneath and found 36 barrels of gunpowder. Then Guy Fawkes was tortured to give away the Gunpowder Plot, and he and his fellow conspirators were brutally executed.

The Puritans

The laws on religion were just as strict for the Puritans. They were very strict Protestants who thought the Church of England services were too much like those of the Catholic Church. They wanted a pure religion. This is why they were called Puritans. They did not like having bishops in the Church of England and priests wearing special robes. They wanted church services to be plain and simple and more like meetings with long sermons.

The Puritans did not believe in pleasure or fine clothes and wore dark garments and tall, cone-shaped hats. They banned music in church, did not believe in enjoying Christmas and stopped working completely on Sundays. This caused much amusement, and someone said a Puritan would "hang his cat on Monday for killing a mouse on Sunday." But although they were often uncomfortable to live with, they were very hard-working, thrifty people.

Although they were often punished for their beliefs, the Puritans did not believe in allowing people to follow any religion they chose. They thought the Puritan way was the only right way, and when they were in power, at the time of Oliver Cromwell, they punished Catholics, Quakers, and anyone else who disagreed with them.

The Pilgrim Fathers

In 1620 a group of strict Puritans (later called the Pilgrim Fathers) decided that the only way to get the freedom they wanted to follow their own religious beliefs was to emigrate to North America.

On 16 September they set sail from Plymouth in the tiny ship 'Mayflower'. Despite many hardships, all but two of the passengers survived the hard Atlantic crossing. They were sea-sick, desperately overcrowded, cold, uncomfortable and hungry, but they sang hymns and psalms to keep their spirits up. Strong gales blew the ship off course and instead of arriving on the warm shores of Virginia, which was what they had intended, they landed in the cold north at a spot they called Plymouth Rock.

The first winter was so severe and the hardships of the Puritans so great, that half the settlers died in the first year. The rest stuck it out. They made peace with the local Indians, and an Indian brave, called Squanto taught them how to grow Indian corn (maize), how to get syrup from the maple tree, how to fish and how to trap wild animals for their skins and furs.

That autumn they reaped their first harvest, and were so overjoyed that they held a Thanksgiving Dinner. Their colony went from strength to strength, and by 1640 about 25,000 settlers were living there. They called it New England.

A Puritan service

The landing of the Pilgrim Fathers in 1620

Things To Do

1. Draw a sequence of pictures to tell the story of the Pilgrim Fathers, from their departure from Plymouth in September 1620 in the 'Mayflower', to the time of the first Thanksgiving Dinner in November 1621.

2. How did the Puritans differ from the Catholics? Did they have anything in common with the Catholics?

3. Why did the Gunpowder Plot fail? Were the Gunpowder Plotters right to try to use violence?

Afterwards

Religious differences caused most of the wars and disturbances in Britain in the Stuart period. One reason for the English Civil War was because the Archbishop of Canterbury tried to force the Scots to change their church services. In 1678 many innocent people were killed because Titus Oates falsely said there was a Catholic plot to kill the King. In 1685 the Duke of Monmouth, a Protestant, tried to overthrow James II, a Catholic. Many people were executed for their part in this rebellion. In 1688 James, himself, was forced to leave the country. The new King William III and his wife Mary were Protestants.

The English Civil War

Roundheads and Cavaliers

It wasn't as if John Hampden was poor and unable to pay the £1 the King's tax collectors demanded. Indeed he was a wealthy landowner, and the £1 needed to pay for the King's ships was something he could easily afford.

But in 1637, John Hampden was sticking up for his rights and those of other people in Britain. He said that because Parliament had not agreed to the tax, the King's men had no right to ask for it. The reason why this agreement had not been given was the King's own fault – he had ruled since 1629 without calling Parliament.

John Hampden was really telling the King, that if he wanted to raise money to govern the country, he had to get the agreement of Parliament first.

Although Hampden lost his case in court, several judges agreed with him. So three years later when Charles needed money for his army, he decided to call another Parliament. But when they met, the members of Parliament were in no mood to give the King money without first getting him to put right their grievances. They wanted to meet regularly in future; not just to be called out whenever the King was short of funds.

Charles decided to show them who was King. He went with some soldiers to the Houses of Parliament to arrest John Hampden and four other members of Parliament, but they were warned in advance. When Charles arrived at Westminster, he found that the five members had gone.

Fearing that the King might use force against them, Parliament decided to take control of the army. Charles refused to agree to this, and on 22nd August 1642 declared war on Parliament.

Statue of John Hampden

King Charles I tries to arrest the five members of Parliament

King Charles I

The first battle of the Civil War was fought at Edgehill in Warwickshire, on a cold day in October 1642. The action began when the King's nephew, Prince Rupert, led the Royal cavalry at the gallop; and the sight of these dashing soldiers on horseback, charging at full pelt with drawn swords, completely routed the inexperienced horsemen fighting for Parliament.

Rupert chased them off the battlefield, but while he was away the remaining Parliamentary soldiers attacked the King's infantry (foot soldiers) and very nearly won the battle. Rupert came back just in time to stop the Parliamentary forces winning.

Oliver Cromwell was so disappointed at the performance of the Parliamentary soldiers, he trained a special force of horsemen (Cromwell's Ironsides) to stand up to these cavalry charges without flinching. The Royalist cavalry also had a nick-name – the Cavaliers – and this soon became the name for all supporters of the King. In their turn, the forces of Parliament were called Roundheads, because some of the Puritan soldiers kept their hair cut short.

The battle of Naseby

The Cavaliers and Roundheads fought battles all over England in the years between 1642 and 1645. The Puritans, townspeople, and people of the south and east mostly supported Parliament, while Anglicans, Catholics, and people in the north and west supported the King.

It was a terrible time. Many people changed sides; some soldiers deserted, whilst others were unwilling to fight away from their homes. Fathers and sons and brothers fought on different sides. Other people could not make up their minds. Some Cavaliers for example, thought that Parliament was right, but could not bring themselves to fight against their King.

Because Parliament had more money and the support of the navy, the King found it hard to get help from outside England. To add to his difficulties, Parliament made an agreement with the Scots, and Scottish soldiers helped to defeat the Cavaliers at the battle of Marston Moor in July 1644.

After Marston Moor, Cromwell formed the New Model Army, with professional soldiers, and on 14th June 1645 they met the Cavaliers at Naseby in Northamptonshire.

The battle started with another brilliant charge, led by Prince Rupert and the cavalry. But foolishly they chased the Roundheads as far as the town of Naseby and then raided the Roundhead supply lines. While they were gone, Cromwell launched a ferocious attack on the Royalist forces, forcing Charles to retreat. By the time Rupert came back, the Royalists were utterly defeated. It was the end of the Civil War.

Then Charles I was taken prisoner by the Roundheads. At first they did not think of killing him, but when he tried to get the Scots to help him, Parliament decided to put the King on trial.

Charles defended himself with dignity and great courage, saying that Parliament had no right to try him, but in the end was found guilty of treason and sentenced to death.

On 30th January 1649, a bitterly cold winter's day, Charles I, King of England, walked through St. James's Park towards Whitehall to the beating of drums. At 2 p.m. he climbed on to the scaffold, where the executioner in a black mask was waiting. Charles put his head on the block and then the axe fell. Someone in the crowd said "there was such a groan by the thousands then present, as I never heard before and desire I may never hear again."

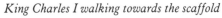
King Charles I walking towards the scaffold

Oliver Cromwell

Oliver Cromwell and the Commonwealth

The Scots were furious at the news of the King's execution, and supported the claims of Prince Charles (later King Charles II). They were defeated by Cromwell at Dunbar and later at Worcester. Charles only managed to escape after hiding in an oak tree.

Parliament now ruled the country but Cromwell was so annoyed at their lack of efficiency that he took charge himself and went to Parliament crying, "You are no Parliament, I say you are no Parliament, I will put an end to your sitting." He then sent them away.

So Cromwell became more powerful than Charles had ever been. He now ruled as Lord Protector and was really dictator of Britain.

During this time, known as the *Commonwealth*, the Puritans, who did not believe in having decorations in a church, sent round soldiers to pull down statues in churches and destroy pictures of religious scenes. They prevented people from going to services on Christmas Day, stopped music in churches, closed the theatres and ended all dancing, bear-baiting and cock-fighting.

Everyone got fed up with this. When Cromwell died there was no one to take his place, so messengers went to the exiled Prince Charles, asking him to come back as King. He made a triumphal return to London as Charles II in 1660.

Cromwell sends Parliament away

Things To Do

1. Look at the famous painting at the top of the page. Write a story to say what you think might have led up to the scene shown in this picture.

2. Draw a sequence of pictures to show how the Civil War started, what happened at Edgehill and Naseby, and finally what happened after the War. Write a sentence under each picture to say what it shows.

3. Would you have supported the Roundheads or the Cavaliers? Write a few sentences to say what choice you would have made if you had been living in England at the time of the Civil War.

Afterwards

Charles II was a pleasure-loving king. His reign was quite different from the Commonwealth under Cromwell. The theatres and bear-baiting pits opened, and people were free to enjoy themselves once again. Some of the men responsible for the death of Charles I were executed, but other supporters of Cromwell were allowed to live peacefully and without punishment. But religion still troubled the country because Charles II had no children and his brother James, a Catholic, was heir to the throne. A group of Protestants called *Whigs* unsuccessfully tried to stop James succeeding to the throne when Charles died. The King's supporters were called *Tories*.

Daily Life in Stuart Britain

John Evelyn

A coach, pulled by six horses, rattled over the cobblestones and entered the country town of Newmarket in Suffolk. John Evelyn got down from the coach and looked with interest at the town, which was packed with people.

After spending the night in a friend's house he joined the thousands of spectators, including Charles II and his courtiers, on the racecourse. "I was on the heath, where I saw the great match run between Woodcock and Flatfoot belonging to the King," he wrote in his diary.

After the race meeting he went to stay at a country mansion nearby. "In the morning, we went hunting and hawking; in the afternoon to cards and dice; thus idly passing the time". John Evelyn was disgusted to see the King's followers "racing, dancing, feasting and revelling".

He wrote his diary from about 1640 to 1700, and his day-to-day comments, and those of Samuel Pepys, in his famous diary, tell us a lot about daily life in Britain at the time of Charles II.

The King and his courtiers sometimes seemed only to live for pleasure. People called Charles "the merry monarch" and he was often seen hunting, playing tennis, skating or sledging. He also liked gambling and going to the theatre.

The ordinary people enjoyed themselves too. Apprentices and young men played football, kicking "a leather ball about as big as one's head, filled with wind"; whilst cock-fighting, bear-baiting and bull-baiting were popular sports once again, after having been banned by the Puritans. Evelyn said they were "barbarous cruelties."

A coffee house in the eighteenth century

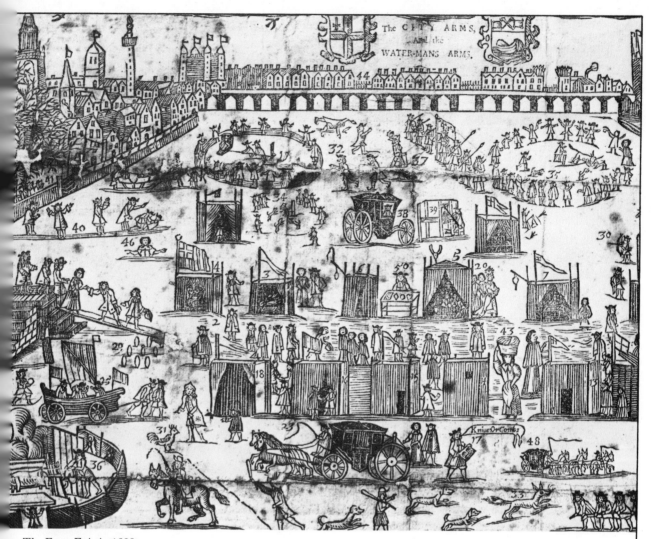

The Frost Fair in 1683

People flocked to fairs like St. Bartholomew's at Smithfield in London, where sweetmeats, fruits, ribbons and trinkets were sold. Pickpockets and thieves jostled with the crowds gaping at the jugglers, acrobats, rope-dancers, strong men and fire-eaters.

In 1683 London had an extra treat when the Thames froze over at Christmas, and rows of canvas stalls were set up on the ice. At this Frost Fair you could buy hot food and drinks. Some people skated or sledged, and some took coach trips on the frozen river.

The Stuart period also saw the coming of coffee houses, where you could buy coffee, tea, or chocolate. Samuel Pepys had his first cup of tea in 1660, and his first cup of "jocolatte", as he called it, in 1664. The coffee houses were meeting places where people could talk over a cup of coffee and a pipeful of tobacco. But the Puritans criticised them and said they were places of "tittle tattle and gossip for fops, pickpockets and foolish citizens."

The streets in the towns were still dark and narrow and the upper floors of the houses jutted out over the streets, making them dull and gloomy. There were no street lights, and at night rich people paid to have a boy light the way for them with a flaming torch.

Drains were poor and rubbish filled the gutters, but some improvements were made. In 1613 a new fresh water supply came to London along the New River. Water carriers sold it in the streets in long wooden buckets, shouting "Any New River water here?"

London, like most towns, was still close to the country, and cows grazed in the centre of the city. Chelsea, Woolwich and Paddington were country villages.

There were no policemen. Samuel Pepys, writing in his diary late at night on 16th January 1660, said the bellman had just come past crying "Past one of the clock, and a cold, frosty, windy morning." Pepys went to bed then, but left his "wife and the maid a-washing still."

Like most well-to-do people, Samuel Pepys had a number of servants. He paid them less in a year, than the cost of one of the wigs on his head. In those days men thought it fashionable to wear long wigs. They cut their own hair very close so that the wig fitted comfortably.

Rich people's clothes were made from silk, velvet, lace and brightly-coloured cloths. Men often wore highly decorated coats and breeches with frills on them. Women wore very full, low-cut gowns with ribbons and lace-trimmings. By contrast the Puritans wore dark clothes with white collars, and poor people wore plain clothes made from coarse woollen cloth.

Samuel Pepys loved buying clothes and kept up with the latest fashions. When his wife, who was in the country, desired "a new petticoat of the new silk striped stuff" he "went to Paternoster Row, and bought her one, with Mr. Creed's help, a very fine rich one, the best I did see there."

Traffic in the streets had changed since the time of the Tudors. The *sedan chair*, a carriage suspended on two poles carried by two chairmen, one at the front and one at the back, was first seen in London in about 1635. Sedan chairs were very useful, because they could be taken up narrow alleyways where a coach could not go. There had been few horse-drawn carriages in medieval times, and then only for the very rich. Now they were often seen in the streets.

A street in Stuart times

A farmhouse in East Anglia

Although most people still worked in the countryside on farms, there were more industries now. Some factory-owners were beginning to use coal instead of wood, because many of the forests had been chopped down to build houses and wooden ships. They called it sea coal, because it was carried in sailing boats from the coalfields of Northumberland and Durham.

The iron-makers still used only wood, and they were very short of timber to turn into charcoal for their blast furnaces. Some had had to build furnaces in forests a long way from the towns.

The manufacture of woollen cloth was very important now in Norfolk, Halifax and Devon. But it was still a home industry where spinners spun yarn for use by weavers in cottages.

Farming had not changed much since Tudor times, but in East Anglia expert Dutch engineers were draining the fens. They dug long ditches and channels to help the water to drain away from waterlogged land. Windmills were used to pump the water off the low land.

There was a lot of interest now in science and in machines, and several great scientists, including Sir Isaac Newton (who discovered the law of gravity), made important discoveries during the Stuart period.

Things To Do

1. Look at the picture on pages 36–37, showing a street scene in London in Stuart times. Imagine you are a foreigner, seeing London for the first time. Write a description of this street.

2. Why do you think the Puritans criticised the coffee houses? What do you think the Puritans thought about Charles II and his courtiers?

3. What changes had taken place in the towns since the time of Queen Elizabeth I (see pages 10–17)?

Afterwards

Industry changed when water, and later steam, were used to make power for machines. Farmers used new machines on their land, tried new crops (like turnips) and divided the land into small fields with hedges - like fields today. Better transport was needed for the growing industries; so many canals were dug for barges to carry heavy goods cheaply. Road transport improved when toll roads, called *turnpikes*, were built. The toll paid by the travellers was used to pay for the upkeep of the road surface.

Horse and cart in about 1675

The Plague

On Sunday 3rd September 1665 the Plague was at its
height in London. Samuel Pepys wrote in his diary on
that day about a shopkeeper, whose family had been
struck down with the disease.

Like all buildings which had Plague in them, the house
had been locked up with the family inside, and "Lord
have mercy on us" had been painted on the door, next
to a large red cross warning other people to keep away.
In desperation, the shopkeeper saved the life of his last
living child by passing her through a window into the
arms of a friend.

The Plague-ridden streets of London

On that same day a tailor called George Vicars, living in the Derbyshire village of Eyam, opened a package of old clothes which had been sent from London. The following day he started to shiver, and then reddish blotches appeared on his body. He died of the Plague on 7th September, and by then others in the village had fallen ill.

Within a month 28 people died of the Plague in Eyam. To stop it spreading further the rector, William Mompesson, persuaded the villagers not to leave Eyam, or contact outsiders in any way.

Despite terrible suffering they stuck it out, and neighbouring tradesmen left them food and other necessities on the edge of the village. The coins they left in payment were washed in vinegar first.

In October 1666, when the Plague had gone, only 88 of the 350 villagers of Eyam were still left alive. Katherine Mompesson, the vicar's wife, had also died.

The Plague was carried by fleas on the rats which thrived in the sewers and gutters of London's dirty, narrow streets. In those days people did not know what caused the disease or how it could be cured.

But they did know that there was less chance of catching the Plague in the countryside. Samuel Pepys sent his wife into the country; and thousands of people fled from London on horseback, in waggons and in carriages. But they carried the disease with them, so that places on the outskirts of London also suffered from the Plague as well as the city. The poor, who could not afford to escape, remained behind in the Plague-ridden streets. So too, did Samuel Pepys.

Inside a house affected by the Plague

So many died they had to be buried in huge graves, called plague pits. The men who had the thankless job of burying the Plague victims went through the deserted streets of the City with a cart, ringing a handbell and crying "Bring out your dead!"

Sometimes mistakes happened. A drunken musician woke up from his stupor to find himself in the back of a dead cart. Alarmed by what he saw, he cried out. You can imagine the shock of the driver when a voice from the back asked "Where am I?"

It was difficult to find a doctor or nurse to attend to anyone with the Plague, because most of them had also fled from the city. Those who remained knew there was little they could do. They wore masks to protect themselves, and carried spices and herbs in the belief that the fragrance would clean the air.

The nursery rhyme "Ring a ring a roses" was sung at this time. People who got the disease had rose-coloured rings of spots (*Ring a ring a roses*), carried herbs and flowers to ward off the disease (*A pocket full of posies*), developed colds and fevers (*Atishoo! Atishoo!*) and the Plague almost always resulted in death (*We all fall down*).

In London the number of Plague deaths only started to go down when colder weather came. On 10th November Mrs Pepys returned, and by then the shops which had been closed were open for business once again.

Pepys was appalled to see so many mounds of fresh earth in the churchyards where some of the Plague victims were buried. As many as 100,000 people may have died in London from the Plague, out of a total population of about 500,000.

Things To Do

1. Londoners, who fled to the country to escape the Plague, were sometimes met by country people, armed with pitch forks, who barred their way. Why do you think they did this? Why didn't the Londoners stay at home like the people of Eyam? What would you have done?

2. What can you see in the picture on pages 40–41? Imagine you are living in London at the time of the Plague. Write a letter to a friend in the countryside, saying what it is like to live in London at this time.

3. The picture below shows a Plague scene – drawn by an artist who lived at the time. Write two or three sentences to say what you can see in this picture.

Afterwards

The Plague came back again, but never with the same terrible effect as in 1665–66. Londoners had still not recovered from the effects of the disease when a great fire burned down a large part of the City in September 1666. The Great Fire had one good effect; it cleared London of many of its old houses and narrow back streets, killing off rats and destroying the filthy gutters and sewers where the Plague rats flourished.

Londoners escaping from the Plague

The Great Fire of London

1st September 1666. The hot dry summer was almost over, and the strong breeze reminded the bellman, walking along Eastcheap on that Saturday night, that autumn would soon be here. Had he checked the bakery in Pudding Lane soon after midnight, he might have saved London from disaster. But at about 2 a.m. the crackling of burning wood and the pungent, stinging smell of smoke, woke Thomas Farriner and his family and servants. Their bakery and house were on fire.

They escaped by climbing on to the roof of the next house, but a panic-stricken maid died when the fire tore through the upper floors of the timber house. Soon the whole row in Pudding Lane was alight and the flames burned fiercely, fanned by the wind.

Six streets away in Seething Lane, Samuel Pepys was woken up by his maid. "Jane called us up about three in the morning, to tell us of a great fire they saw in the City. So I rose and went to her window. I thought it far enough off; and so went to bed again and to sleep."

When he got up on Sunday morning he thought the fire had died down. But he was wrong. "By and by Jane comes and tells me that she hears that above 300 houses have been burned down tonight by the fire we saw and that it is now burning down all Fish-street by London Bridge."

In order to get a better view Pepys got into his boat and rowed up the Thames to London Bridge. To his amazement, little effort was being made to put the fire out. Instead, everybody was trying to get their possessions into carts in the streets. Even pigeons burned their wings before moving on.

Although there were no fire brigades, the householders had fire buckets and the watchmen had squirts which could spray water on to the flames. If all else failed, the houses immediately in danger from the fire could be pulled down, to make a gap which would stop the flames spreading further.

Pepys went to Whitehall and urged the King to do something, saying that "unless His Majesty did command houses to be pulled down nothing could stop the fire." Charles II acted at once, and told Pepys to go to Sir Thomas Bludworth, the Lord Mayor "and command him to spare no houses". So Pepys hurried back, and caught up with the Lord Mayor "in Canning Street, like a man spent, with a handkerchief about his neck."

The Lord Mayor had, in fact, been called out in the early hours to the fire, but had thought it a small affair. Now he was in a panic. "Lord! What can I do? I am spent; people will not obey me. I have been pulling down houses; but the fire overtakes us faster than we can do it." Pepys noted with anxiety the many goods in warehouses near the fire, such as oil, wine, pitch and tar, all of which would burn easily.

The Great Fire of London

Samuel Pepys

After dinner Pepys took his boat "so near the fire as we could for smoke; and all over the Thames, with one's face in the wind, you were almost burned with a shower of fire-drops." At night it became spectacular, "a most horrid malicious flame, not like the fine flame of an ordinary fire. It made me weep to see it."

That night Pepys got his things together and took them in a cart to Bethnal Green "riding myself in my night-gown in the cart; and Lord! to see how the streets and the highways are crowded with people running and riding."

For three or four days the fire raged, burning down a large part of London. By Wednesday the wind dropped and the Great Fire died down. 500 streets, 13,000 houses, 89 churches and St. Paul's Cathedral had been destroyed. Thousands had no homes. Coming so soon after the Plague, it was seen by some Puritans as God's punishment on the people for spending too much time on pleasure.

Soon wide new streets of brick and stone houses were put up. Wooden houses and thatched roofs were not allowed, and the new houses did not jut out over the roadway like the old timber ones; so the risk of fire spreading was less. There were new underground sewers. London was a cleaner, healthier and safer place to live in.

Firemark

Things To Do

1. Draw a sequence of pictures to tell the story of the Great Fire of London. Write a sentence under each picture to say what it shows.

2. Write a description of the view of the Great Fire seen in the picture on pages 44–45. Try to make your account as vivid and colourful as possible, so that anyone reading your description will be able to imagine what it was like at that time.

3. What were the causes of the Great Fire? Was anyone to blame?

4. How did the Great Fire help to make London a better place in which to live?

Afterwards

Londoners now realised how dangerous fire was. Some insured their homes with insurance companies, and were given special firemarks to display. Each insurance company formed its own fire brigade, and when they saw a fire, they checked the firemark first to see that the house was insured by their company. If not, they left it to burn! These firemarks can still be seen on some houses today.

One big problem was what to do about St. Paul's Cathedral. It was decided to pull down the ruins, and a new cathedral was designed and built by Sir Christopher Wren. Wren also designed the Monument to the fire, which was built close to Pudding Lane, where the fire broke out.

Sir Christopher Wren

At Home and Abroad

The Jacobite Rebellions

The chieftain of the MacDonalds of Glencoe urged his horse forward into the driving snow. The only thing that kept him going was the threat the King's men had made, that soldiers would treat the MacDonalds as enemies if they failed to take the oath in time. This was because all the clans (families) living in the Scottish Highlands had been ordered to swear their loyalty to King William by 31st December 1691.

Now, because of the blizzard, he was two days late. Luckily the Sheriff in Inveraray let him take the oath, and the chieftain breathed a sigh of relief.

Massacre at Glencoe

Bonnie Prince Charlie – the Young Pretender

But in Edinburgh, the King's minister in Scotland was looking for an excuse to teach the hated Highlanders a lesson. His chance had come at last, and he sent an army captain, together with 120 Scottish soldiers (mostly members of the Campbell Clan), to attack their sworn enemies, the MacDonalds of Glencoe.

When they reached the Glencoe valley, they told the MacDonalds they came as friends and needed shelter. For a fortnight they were given food and friendship. Then one bitterly cold morning, while it was still dark, they treacherously broke into the homes of the Mac-Donalds and shot all the men, women and children they could find.

The sound of gunfire aroused the other members of the Clan and they escaped into the hills, leaving 38 MacDonalds massacred in the valley. It was not something the Highlanders would forget in a hurry.

Fifteen years later, in the reign of Queen Anne, England and Scotland were joined together as one nation by the Act of Union.

When Anne died in 1714, the English invited George I, a Protestant prince from Hanover in Germany, to be king. They did not ask James Edward, the Catholic son of James II. Many Highlanders were Catholics and rallied to the side of the Old Pretender, as he was later called, when rebellion broke out in 1715. But British soldiers soon crushed the revolt and James went back into exile in France.

Thirty years later, his son Charles tried again. Bonnie Prince Charlie (known as the Young Pretender) was a dashing young man with plenty of charm. He landed in northern Scotland in 1745 with a handful of men, and soon hundreds of clansmen rallied to his standard and marched southwards with him into England. But during the long march Charles's soldiers became tired and discouraged, and many left him. When they reached Derby, the Scottish army turned back.

The English armies gave chase and wiped out the Highland army at the battle of Culloden Moor on 16th April 1746. The clansmen fought with great courage but were no match for the British soldiers. Afterwards many Highlanders were captured and killed.

Charles fled to Europe, helped by a young girl called Flora MacDonald. He had no children, so at last there were no more Stuarts to claim the throne.

The Four Georges

George I became king in 1714 because Parliament did not want the Stuarts, who were Catholics, to succeed to the throne. George spoke German, not English. He let Sir Robert Walpole, his chief adviser, rule the country as Britain's first prime minister in his place.

Walpole believed that Britain should become a great trading nation. In India, the East India Company had built many trading settlements and forts, and had started an army of Indians, called *sepoys* to defend them.

France, Britain's enemy in the 18th century, supported the armies of the Indian princes against the British. In 1757, during the reign of George II, Robert Clive won a great victory at Plassey over a much larger Indian army which was helped by the French. So the French were defeated in India, which became part of the British Empire.

Two years later the French army in North America was beaten by General Wolfe at Quebec. The French commanded the Heights overlooking the St Lawrence river, so Wolfe daringly landed 4,000 soldiers at night. They climbed the steep cliffs and defeated the French the following day. This victory made sure Canada would stay British.

In 1760 George III succeeded his grandfather, George II, and made peace with France. George was a stubborn man and wanted to have a bigger say in the affairs of the government. When the American colonists rebelled in 1775 he would not agree to their complaints; and so in the end he lost the American colonies altogether. His son later became George IV in 1820.

The American War of Independence

America had grown into an important country by the eighteenth century and sent many goods to Britain. Among them were cotton and tobacco, which were grown on plantations in the hot lands of the south, using slave labour.

The colonies were part of the British Empire, but by this time they looked after themselves most of the time. So when in 1765, the British government tried to make them pay a new tax, they objected. They said that since the American colonies had no members of Parliament in London, it was not right that they should have to pay. The British also made them buy expensive tea from the East India Company, when they could get cheap tea from other places; and the Americans did not like this either.

In 1773 a group of Americans, disguised as Red Indians, crept on board a British ship in Boston harbour and threw 342 crates of tea into the sea. They did this to show how much they hated British rule. The British were furious, and fighting soon began. On 4th July 1776 the Americans made a Declaration of Independence, saying they were no longer ruled by Britain.

In the long war which followed, the Americans often seemed to be losing. But in the end their leader, George Washington, forced Lord Cornwallis, the British commander, to surrender at Yorktown in 1781, and the United States became an independent nation at last.

The Boston Tea Party

The Discovery of Australia and New Zealand

On 25th August 1768, the ship *Endeavour*, commanded by Captain James Cook, sailed out of Plymouth harbour on an epic voyage to the Pacific Ocean. From the island of Tahiti, Cook sailed southwards to explore the southern Pacific and, in October 1769, his crew first caught sight of the coast of New Zealand.

Cook decided to make an accurate map of the New Zealand coastline by sailing right round the islands. After that he sailed north-west towards Australia, which was then called New Holland.

No one knew then what the east coast of Australia was like, so in 1770 when they landed there was great interest among the crew about what they would see.

One of the members of the party was a scientist called Joseph Banks. Captain Cook wrote of this first landing in Australia: "The name of Botany Bay was given to this place, from the great number of plants collected by Mr. Banks. The English colours were displayed, and the name of the ship, with the date of the year, was carved in a tree near the place where we landed."

Captain Cook's men also met Aborigines and got their first sight of a boomerang and a kangaroo. Cook claimed Australia for King George III, and then sailed home for Britain with news of the territories he had discovered.

The landing of Captain Cook at Botany Bay

Things To Do

1. Paint or draw a series of pictures to illustrate some of the main events in the story of the Scottish Highlands, from the Massacre of Glencoe in 1692, to the Battle of Culloden in 1746. Write a sentence under each picture to say what it shows.

2. Make a time chart for the 18th century, by copying this list of dates, and writing against each year the name of the important event which happened then:

1707	1714	1715	1745	1746	1757
1759	1760	1765	1770	1773	1775
1776	1781				

3. Write a sentence to say what you know about each of the following:

Captain Cook	General Wolfe
George III	Bonnie Prince Charlie
Joseph Banks	Robert Clive
George Washington	Sir Robert Walpole

Afterwards

Although Britain lost her American colonies after the defeat at Yorktown, she still had Canada. One result was that criminals in Britain could no longer be sent as a punishment to work on American plantations. So they were sent to Australia instead, and in 1788 Botany Bay became the first British convict settlement.

Country Life in the Eighteenth Century

The traveller rubbed her eyes in disbelief. The huge open fields, common lands and meadows had gone. In their place she saw a patchwork of small fields with trim hedges; and six new red-brick farmhouses, each by itself among the fields. Twenty years earlier when she left the district, the farmers lived in the village itself, and their farms were divided into a number of different strips of land, separate from each other among the three open fields.

A stranger told her the full story – how it all began when the richer farmers got together to discuss the latest methods of farming. Most of the improvements they talked about were only possible if all the fields could be put together to make separate farms. The old open fields held them back. As it was they wasted a lot of time going from one strip to another, while lazy neighbours let weeds spread on to their land.

Robert Bakewell (see page 56)

'Turnip' Townsend

Haymaking in newly-enclosed fields

Now at last they could do something about it. Because the richer farmers owned most of the land between them, they managed to get Parliament to pass a law to enclose the village fields. A large number of the poorer villagers were against the idea, but they could do nothing about it.

First of all, the fields of the village were carefully measured by surveyors, who recorded how much land each farmer owned. When the survey was over, the land was shared out among the farmers. The trouble was that the land was not all as good; some fields sloped, some were boggy, and some had poor soils. So some farmers got better farms than others.

The lawyers and the surveyors had to be paid for their work. Each landholder also had to pay to have his fields hedged or walled. This was very expensive and farmers who could not afford to pay had to sell their land. Then, without a farm, they tried to get new jobs as farm labourers. But this was difficult, because the new methods of farming and the new machines sometimes meant that fewer farmworkers were needed now.

Gradually, as more and more villages in Britain were enclosed, the numbers of poor people increased. But the richer farmers did well, and made many improvements to their farming methods.

Separate fields helped them to rear pure-bred animals such as Longhorn cattle, Southdown sheep or the New Leicester sheep which Robert Bakewell bred in Leicestershire. The farmers used fertilisers in their fields and grew new root crops (such as turnips and swedes) and grass crops like clover and lucerne.

In the past farmers found they got better crops if they left a field fallow (without anything growing in it) every third year. But in the eighteenth century they discovered they could get just as good crops every year, if they followed a four-year crop rotation (a different crop each year): wheat in year 1, a root crop in year 2, barley in year 3 and a grass crop like clover in year 4.

Gin gang

The farmers brought in new machinery, such as the Rotherham plough, which was easier to use. A farmer called Jethro Tull invented a seed drill in 1701 to sow corn in rows, so that the land could be weeded with a horse-drawn hoe.

Some farmers built a gin gang shed to house a wheel turned by four horses, which provided the power for a thrashing machine.

Many other improvements were made. Some farmers drained marshy land; some planted trees. Thomas Coke of Holkham in Norfolk was one of the men who made the new methods well-known; and Lord Townsend was so keen on root crops that he was nicknamed "Turnip" Townsend.

We know what life was like in an eighteenth-century village from the books of travellers and from letters and diaries.

Gilbert White lived in the village of Selborne in Hampshire, and said it had one long straggling street, which was so narrow that carts could only pass in certain places. Most of the village people were farmworkers. "We abound with poor," he wrote. "Many are sober and industrious, and live comfortably in good stone or brick cottages." Unlike other villages, the houses all had glass windows, and there were no "mud buildings."

The village green, near the church, was the centre of village life in Selborne. In summer the adults sat gossiping under a tree, whilst the children played games. On May 1st they danced round the maypole, until it blew down in a gale.

Little Walsingham, Norfolk

Gilbert White

Most village maypoles have gone, but other features of eighteenth-century village life can often be seen, such as the cage – a small building where prisoners were locked-up until they could be brought to trial. For minor crimes, wrongdoers sat with their legs fastened in the village stocks.

Large villages often had a market, for in those days, people had to buy most of the things they needed within walking distance of their homes. This is why they also had many more shops than you see today. Most villages also had the workshops of the local blacksmith, wheelwright, carpenter and saddler.

The high spot of the countryman's year was the visit of the fair to the local market town. At Sherborne in Dorset, Pack Monday Fair was held in the middle of October. It began when the clock struck midnight and the boys of the town paraded through the streets, blowing horns and pipes.

A hiring fair

The next day the fair was soon well under way with barkers shouting "Walk up, walk up, ladies and gentlemen! The price is only two pence." One stallholder raffled gingerbread, a man "sporting a worn-out wig and huge spectacles" sold razors, knives and scissors, and you could ride a horse or in a coach on "Mr. Warr's merry roundabout".

At hiring fairs, farmworkers and servants tried to get work. At one fair "a waggoner, or ploughboy, had a piece of whipcord in his hat; a cowman had some cow hair; a shepherd had wool; a gardener had flowers. The girls wishing to be hired were in a spot apart from the men and boys, and all stood like cattle at a fair waiting for dealers."

Being a maidservant was often the only job a girl could get. It was hard work. One country lady expected her maid to cook, do the washing, clean the house, make the beds, milk the cows and "when she has done her work she sits down to spin."

Jethro Tull's seed drill

Things To Do

1. Look at the photograph on page 57 showing the village of Little Walsingham in Norfolk. Draw a picture to show this village scene as it might have looked two hundred years ago, with a deeply rutted and muddy road running through the village, and carts and horses in the village square.

2. Write a sentence to say what you know about each of the following:

Lord Townsend   Jethro Tull
Robert Bakewell   Thomas Coke

3. What were the advantages and disadvantages of enclosing the open fields? Was it fair to the poor farmer? Was it necessary do you think? Write an account of what happened when the open fields in a village were enclosed.

Afterwards

The changes in farming took place at the same time as changes in industry (pages 60–65) and in transport (pages 72–77). In the past many farmworkers' families had been able to make ends meet by spinning yarn or weaving cloth in their cottages. Machines in factories meant that their work was no longer needed. At the same time it was more difficult than ever to get jobs on the land. Many people were reduced to poverty, and many country people left the villages for the fast growing factory towns.

The Growth of Industry

A column of smoke from the mine chimney helped the Frenchman, called Saint Fond, find his way to the coal mine he was visiting near Newcastle-upon-Tyne. When at last he got there, a large steam engine was rattling and spluttering, as it pumped out water from the pit shaft and helped to draw fresh air into the coal mine deep below the ground.

Saint Fond learned that the colliery employed 70 miners at the coal face, and a further 30 people on the surface loading coal into waggons and doing other jobs.

To get down to the coal seam, the miners had to go down one of the two pit shafts on a wooden board which hung from two ropes (like a garden swing) and a chain. Two miners sat on the board facing each other, gripping the chain, and were lowered to the bottom of the shaft by the horse gin on top. This was two horses turning a large wheel which unwound the chain.

A coal mine in about 1780

At the bottom they had to stoop to walk to the coal face through narrow tunnels held up by wooden pit props. In places they had to crawl on their hands and knees. From time to time a coal tub went by, pulled on an underground railway track by women or children, bent double with the weight.

Now and then along these tunnels there were wooden gates, and at each a young child of 7 or 8 sat patiently in the dark, opening it to let the waggons through.

At the coal face men stripped to the waist hacked at the coal with pick-axes. Around them there were deep pools of water. The mine would have flooded but for the steam engine on the surface pumping the water away. The pump used in the colliery had been invented by Thomas Newcomen in 1712.

Falls of rock in the tunnels were common. Miners were often killed or crippled. The worst accidents happened when underground gas exploded. In those days the miners had no safety lamps, and no electricity, and could only see with the aid of candles and oil lamps. To keep the air fresh, the miners kept a blazing fire going under one of the two shafts – this caused a draught but blew away musty air and helped the miners to breathe easily. Unhappily, the fire sometimes caught the gas as well, and then there was an explosion.

The coal was wound up the shaft in baskets which were tipped into waggons on the surface, and pulled by horses down a gently sloping railway to the coal ships waiting on the river Tyne, some distance away. More and more coal was being used, for many industries were using it as a fuel.

Coalbrookdale

Some experiments had been made to use coal, instead of charcoal, to smelt iron ore, but it was not successfully used until 1709, when Abraham Darby baked coal in an oven to make coke, and then used it in his furnaces to smelt iron ore.

Darby's blast furnaces at Coalbrookdale in Shropshire looked exciting at night when the flames lit up the night sky. A traveller wrote about "the noise of the forges and mills with all their vast machinery, the flames bursting from the furnaces with the burning of the coal and the smoke of the lime kilns." Over 1,000 people worked at Coalbrookdale, many living in houses specially built by the Darby family for their workers.

There were still many small forges and furnaces with waterwheels operating tilt hammers (see page 14).

At that time there was a growing need for good iron to make the new machines in the cotton and woollen mills and for the new steam engines.

For hundreds of years weavers and spinners had worked by hand in their own homes, selling each week's work to a clothier. Now all this changed.

Thomas Lombe built a silk mill five storeys high, with 600 workers, by the river Derwent in Derby in 1719, so that he could use a waterwheel to power his silk spinning machines.

Spinning jenny

In 1733 John Kay invented the *flying shuttle* to help speed up the weaving of woollen cloth, for it enabled one weaver to do the work of two, and it made better cloth. By 1760 most weavers were using it. What was needed now was a machine which would speed up the spinning of the yarn.

A Blackburn cotton worker, called James Hargreaves, got the idea for a spinning machine when he saw an overturned spinning wheel on its side. His *spinning jenny*, as he called it, turned eight spindles at once instead of one. At first he used it in his own home; but, needing money, he had to sell a number of his machines. Some spinners, alarmed that the spinning jenny would throw them out of work, stormed his house in 1768 and destroyed his spinning jenny.

But they could not stop progress. Already Richard Arkwright had an idea for a new type of spinning machine, and put one together in a room at Preston Grammar School. But he was worried that the cotton workers would smash up his machine like Hargreaves', and moved from Lancashire to Derbyshire.

Cotton weavers breaking into the home of John Kay to smash his flying shuttle

At work inside a cotton mill in about 1780

There, in 1771, he built the first cotton mill at Cromford by the river Derwent. He had to have water power because his machine was too heavy to work by hand. It produced a stronger thread than the spinning jenny, and was so successful that other manufacturers also built water-powered spinning mills.

Soon the hand spinners in the cottages were out of work and had to get jobs in the mills. They were mainly women workers. An onlooker, seeing them stream out of a mill, said they were pale and thin and covered with flecks of cotton thread.

Many mill-owners began to employ young children in their mills, as well as adults, because they could make them work hard for long hours and low wages. The children were beaten if they went to sleep at work.

In 1788 steam engines were used for the first time to power machines, and shortly afterwards a power loom was invented. Soon many hand-loom weavers were put out of work as well, and had to find jobs in factories.

Things To Do

1. Write a story about the first day at work of a young boy or girl at a colliery in the eighteenth century. Describe the steam engine, the pit shaft, the descent to the coal face, the underground railway and the job of opening and shutting the gates to let the waggons through.

2. Draw a sequence of pictures to tell the story of how the cloth industry changed from the handloom weavers and spinners in their cottages in 1700 to the first textile mills and factories a hundred years later. Write a sentence under each picture to say what it shows.

3. Why did some of the workers destroy the new machines? Did they stop new machinery being used in the end?

Afterwards

Many other industries grew up. Josiah Wedgwood became a great manufacturer of pottery in Staffordshire, using local coal to fire his pottery kilns. China clay was brought to his works in Stoke-on-Trent along the newly-opened Trent and Mersey Canal. Wedgwood's pottery was famous for its quality and beauty. Wedgwood also tried hard to improve the conditions of the pottery workers. In most of the new industrial areas workpeople lived in an atmosphere of steam, smoke, ashes, fumes, oil and grease. These new industrial towns grew fast. Crowded streets of small houses with poor drains soon turned into slums.

Pottery made by the first Josiah Wedgwood

Daily Life in a Georgian Town

Street robbery at night

Execution at Tyburn

One winter's night, in Albemarle Street in London, five thieves waited quietly in the dark for a victim. Shortly before 9 p.m. a messenger called Richard Harvey hurried with a letter to the post. While one of the gang kept a lookout for the watchman, the other four jabbed Harvey in the face with a pistol, stole some money and ran off.

A week later they were caught, but not by detectives. Two of the gang gave evidence against the other three. In those days *thief-takers* (who were usually criminals themselves) acted as policemen and arrested criminals for a reward.

Although the three thieves had stolen less than £2, they were hanged. In the 18th century over 200 sorts of crime were punished with death. Lesser crimes were punished with a whipping or perhaps transportation to the American colonies or Australia.

Some wrongdoers were sentenced to stand in the pillory, where they stood with their arms held fast in a wooden board with holes in it, whilst the mob pelted them with rubbish, and sometimes blinded or crippled them with stones.

These were cruel times. Huge crowds gathered at Tyburn (now Marble Arch) to watch the executions. They treated them as an excuse for a day out, and not as a warning against crime.

The crowded houses and alleyways of the slums, where the poor people of London lived, were like a rabbit warren. The streets were so badly lit at night (with a few weak oil lamps) it was not surprising that most criminals escaped.

There were not enough good houses for all the people in the city. Often a poor family had to live in one room with damp, peeling walls, a leaking ceiling, rotten floorboards and broken windows. They had little furniture and their only light came from a candle. They got their water from a tap in the street and carried it home in a bucket. There were no proper lavatories or drains, and the gutters of the darkest alleyways ran with filth and rubbish.

A street in a crowded London slum

Many people wore rags and lived on bread and water. Any spare money from stealing or begging was often spent on gin. It was so cheap that a gin shop advertised: "Drunk for a penny. Dead drunk for tuppence." In fact many people did die from drinking it. Few poor people lived to old age, and most children died before they grew up. Babies were even left to die in the streets. There were few hospitals to care for the huge population, which suffered from poverty and disease.

By contrast, rich people lived in tall elegant houses, often with a low wall at the top to hide the slope of the roof. Steps led down to the basement and were protected by iron railings. The main entrance often had a porch resting on pillars, called a *portico*. By the door there were footscrapers, so that visitors could scrape the mud from their shoes and boots before entering the house.

Inside the house there were rich carpets and fine furniture. Servants kept the house running smoothly.

A fashionable street in a Georgian town

Beau Brummell – a leader of fashion

Most rich people spent their lives eating, drinking, gambling and going to *routs* (parties) and balls. Every year they went to Bath to take the waters. There was a warm spring at Bath, and drinking the water was supposed to be good for you. Bath grew rapidly and soon became well-known as a place where rich and famous people came to enjoy themselves.

The streets in most Georgian towns were made of cobblestones, with pavements at the side protected from traffic by posts called *bollards*. The shops had windows with small panes so that goods could be shown without getting them wet. They were usually open from 8 in the morning to 11 at night. Outside in the busiest shopping streets you could hear the cries of street traders – "Hot spice gingerbread, smoking hot!" and "Pretty Maids! Pretty Pins!"

Although London was much smaller then than today, travelling from one part of the city to another was a problem. Rich people went in their private carriages or by sedan chair. Lesser people could hire hackney carriages or sedan chairs like modern taxis.

The clothes people wore then were often very grand. Women wore powdered wigs piled high on the head. They often put patches on their faces, and used plenty of make-up. Men had wigs too. They wore knee-length breeches with frock coats, and tricorne hats (hats with three corners).

Children from a smart home had a governess to teach them lessons. There were only a few schools for girls, but plenty of boys' schools, including grammar schools. Lessons were usually dull and Latin and Greek were the main subjects. Discipline was very strict, and pupils were beaten for very small reasons.

By this time more and more people had learned to read, and newspapers were being published to keep them up-to-date with the news. But they were very expensive to buy and many people preferred to read the newspapers in the coffee houses instead of buying a copy themselves.

Public executions and whippings were common; and brutal and cruel sports such as bull-baiting and cock-fighting were popular. Crowds flocked to see men fighting with their bare fists. Gentlemen who quarrelled sometimes fought a duel, using swords or pistols.

Cricket first became popular in the eighteenth century. In those days it was played with curved bats, and bowlers bowled underarm.

A fire engine

Cockfighting

Great actors and actresses starred in plays in the theatres. Sarah Siddons and David Garrick were as popular then, as leading film stars are today. Theatres, assembly rooms for dancing, and pleasure gardens were built in the large towns.

Vauxhall Gardens and Ranelagh Gardens were favourite places to go to in London. Visitors could eat in restaurants and cafes, listen to the band, walk through the gardens which were lit up at night with coloured lights, and watch the firework displays and balloon shows.

Rich people began to go to the seaside for holidays. Doctors said it was healthy to bathe in cold sea water; so seaside resorts like Brighton, Weymouth and Scarborough became fashionable.

Sarah Siddons – a leading actress

Things To Do

1. Compare the Georgian streets seen in the pictures on pages 67–69. Make a list of the differences between them. What differences are there between the street on pages 68–69 and a modern street scene?

2. Write a sentence to describe the cockfight shown in the picture opposite.

3. Try to imagine what it must have been like to live in the slums of Georgian London. Write a story of a journey through the slums at that time.

A Bow Street Runner

4. Paint or draw a large poster to depict life in a Georgian town. Include as many different aspects of everyday life then, as you can.

Afterwards

London, like the industrial towns, grew bigger and bigger. A disease called *cholera* spread through the slums in about 1830, and many poor people died. It was caused by bad drains and water.

In 1749 the magistrates at Bow Street Court paid a small group of men to investigate crimes. These *Bow Street Runners*, as they were called, were very successful. Later on a proper police force in London was started. Soon after that London had a fire brigade as well. At about the same time horse buses made it possible for ordinary people to cross London without having to walk all the way.

Travel in the Eighteenth Century

James Woodforde, a country parson, and his niece Nancy were returning home to Norfolk. They drank tea in the Bull Inn in Bishopsgate in London, before going out into the courtyard to occupy the seats they had booked in the *Expedition* coach bound for Norwich. Stage coaches in those days were usually given names like *Tantivy*, *Rocket* and *Tally-ho*.

At about nine in the evening the stage coach was ready in the inn yard. While the four horses were harnessed, Parson Woodforde and Nancy climbed inside the cramped compartment, which seated four passengers. It was cheaper to sit on top of the coach, but the seats were uncomfortable there, and passengers had to face the night air and the worst of the weather.

In the courtyard of a coaching inn

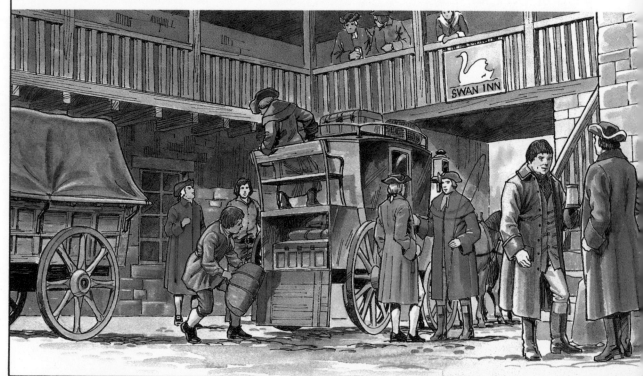

A mail coach passing through a tollgate

At last the coachman got up on to his box at the front of the coach, wrapped his legs in rugs, and took up the four reins in one hand and the whip in the other.

The guard at the back cried "All right, let 'em go" and blew his horn. The coach rolled through the archway tunnel leading from the courtyard to the road (called the *porte cochère*), and soon they were rattling along the cobblestones of the darkened city on the road to Norwich.

The *Expedition* coach, like many other stage and mail coaches, travelled through the night with the aid of two large coach lamps at the front. Fortunately it was a moonlit night and they made good time.

In the early hours of the morning they had breakfast at an inn and stayed there half an hour. The coach services kept to a strict timetable, so innkeepers had no excuse if the horses were not ready, or if the service for meals and hot drinks was slow.

When they travelled on the turnpike roads (see page 75) the guard had to pay a toll to the turnpike keeper at the toll house. Parson Woodforde's journey took about 15 hours for the 170 kilometre journey and they arrived at the Maids Head Inn in Norwich at about 2 p.m. "Thank God safe and well" wrote Parson Woodforde after his journey.

In those days a long road journey was an adventure. The roads were often poor, and the lurching and swaying of the vehicle often made travellers 'coach-sick'. Upstairs passengers sometimes fell off. The seats were uncomfortable, whether the coach was riding on cobblestones in town or over deep-rutted roads in the country. Fortunately there were frequent stops (called *stages*) to change the horses (hence the name stage coach).

The biggest danger for road travellers was armed robbery. There were still many highwaymen about, armed with pistols. They waited at crossroads, under cover, for the lone carriage or stage coach to come along. Passengers learned to fear the sudden jolt as the coach pulled up, and the abrupt command "Stand and deliver!" Some passengers kept some gold coins ready in a special pocket in case of attack by highwaymen.

Highwaymen often found out about passengers from servants working in the coaching inns on the main roads. The coaching inns were built specially for stage coaches and their passengers. You could tell them by the porte cochère at the front of the building, which led to a courtyard at the back.

Tollgate sign

Highwaymen

Inside passengers got down here, but upstairs passengers often had to get down in the main road, to avoid having their hats knocked off when the coach went under the arch.

On arrival at an inn the passengers sometimes only had time to swallow a hot drink brought out to the coach; but at other times got a full meal. It was a cheering sight in winter to see a blazing log fire in the dining room, with tables piled high with hot food.

The owners of private carriages got special attention from the inn landlords. Only the well-to-do could afford to travel by private coach. There were several types of carriage.

Poor people could not afford to ride in the stage coach. If they had to travel a long way, they went in the stage waggon. This was a huge covered cart with four enormous wheels, pulled by as many as eight horses. It lumbered along the country roads at a snail's pace, delivering goods at villages and towns, and carrying thirty or forty passengers packed like cattle in the back.

The stage coach services were only possible because the roads had been improved. Groups of businessmen paid for road repairs with tolls collected from travellers. They built a fence and a gate across the road, and appointed a toll bar keeper to take a toll from every coach or cart passing through, except for the mail coaches which were allowed through by law free of charge.

On a long journey a traveller had to pay tolls at a dozen toll houses or more. Some of these *turnpike roads* as they were called were very good. In general they made travelling in Britain very much easier than it had been since the time of the Romans.

Waggon and horses

Dick Turpin's grave in York

The Duke of Bridgewater

Carrying goods from one part of Britain to another was a serious problem. Some goods were taken by packhorse train – a long line of horses, each carrying two packs, slung on either side. The packhorse drivers did not need to keep to main roads, and could take their horses across the hills over well-worn paths. Narrow packhorse bridges, with high rounded arches, were built to take them across streams.

Stage waggons carried many goods, but were no good for heavy raw materials such as coal and clay. So, from about 1760 until the railways came in 1830, a large number of canals were dug, so that raw materials could be carried cheaply by barge to the new mills and factories.

The most famous of these new waterways was the Bridgewater Canal, built by James Brindley in Lancashire, and opened in 1765. Excited visitors were amazed to see how tunnels sometimes took the canal underground, whilst a special bridge called an *aqueduct*, took it over the River Irwell. The canal was used to carry coal from the Duke of Bridgewater's coal mines to Manchester and Liverpool.

Trade with America and Asia also grew, and merchant ships from all parts of the world could be seen in London, Bristol and Liverpool. Some merchants grew rich on the profits of the African slave trade, taking captured slaves across the Atlantic to work on plantations in America.

The Bridgewater Canal – the aqueduct over the River Irwell

James Brindley

The coming of the railways in the 1830's brought the canal age to a close

Things To Do

1. Would you have enjoyed travelling by stage coach? Write a description of a journey in a stage coach, using your own words to describe the departure from the inn courtyard, changing horses, early morning breakfast, an encounter with highwaymen, going through a tollgate, arrival at an inn.

2. Paint or draw a picture to illustrate the journey made by Parson Woodforde and his niece Nancy in 1786.

3. What were:
   a porte cochère   a toll house   a stage waggon
Write one or two sentences about each of these.

Afterwards

The mail coaches, first introduced in 1784, were fast and very good. They kept to a strict timetable and the guard had to carry a clock with him so that times of arrival and departure could be recorded. There were over 700 mail coaches on the roads by 1830. But in that year the first regular passenger train services were opened between Manchester and Liverpool. The coming of the railway was soon to end the days of the coachman and the canal barge. Rail transport was so much quicker, more convenient for heavy goods, and very much cheaper for passengers.

Index

Acknowledgements

The author and publishers wish to acknowledge the following photograph sources.

BBC Hulton Picture Library p.23 top right, 34 top, 54 left, 69, 70 top, 71 bottom, 74 bottom, 74/75
Bibliothek der Ryksuniversitat Urecht p.15
J Allan Cash Ltd. p.57 top, 75 bottom
Corporation of Bristol p.22
Buckinghamshire County Museum p.28
Mary Evans Picture Library, p.34 bottom, 49 top, 56 bottom
Mansell Collection p.6, 7 top, 14 top, 18 top, 25 top left, 26, 31, 35, 39, 59 top, 63, 70 bottom
                     46 (left and right), 50, 54 top, 71 bottom, 71 top, 76, 77
National Maritime Museum, p.19
National Portrait Gallery, p.4 5 bottom, 7 bottom, 32 top
Rt Hon. The Earl of Pembroke p.29 bottom
Ann Ronan p.47 bottom
Science Museum p.63
By kind permission of the Marquis of Tavistock, and the Trustees of the
   Bedford Estates p.5 top
Universal Tutorial Press Ltd. p.74
Walker Art Gallery p.9, 33
Josiah Wedgwood & Sons Ltd. p.65
All other photographs supplied by the author.

The publishers have made every effort to trace all copyright holders,
but if they have inadvertently overlooked any, they will be pleased to
make the necessary arrangements at the first opportunity.

First published 1982
Published by Macmillan Education Ltd
London and Basingstoke
Associated companies and representatives
throughout the world

Printed in Hong Kong

ISBN 0 333 27520 9

Illustrated by Michael Strand